Original title:
The Whimsical Woodsman

Copyright © 2025 Creative Arts Management OÜ
All rights reserved.

Author: Lorenzo Barrett
ISBN HARDBACK: 978-1-80567-242-5
ISBN PAPERBACK: 978-1-80567-541-9

Sketches in the Shade

In a forest of green where the squirrels giggle,
A fellow with axes would dance and wiggle.
His hat was too big, and his coat was bright,
He'd trip on the roots in the morning light.

With every swing, he'd chop with flair,
Only to find he'd miss the air.
The trees would chuckle, branches would sway,
As he'd stumble about, in his clumsy ballet.

Laughter in the Leaves

Beneath the tall trees, in a cloak of gray,
A jester with logs would often play.
His friends were the birds, who'd sing with glee,
While he tried to balance on a branch like a bee.

With a woosh and a woof, he'd spin around,
Falling like leaves on the soft ground.
The critters would snicker, paws on their sides,
As he rolled like a log through the forest rides.

The Marvelous Misadventures of a Log-Cutter

Once a cutter with spirit, so brave and so bold,
Set off for the woods with stories untold.
His aim was to carve a grand piece of art,
But his effort went sideways—oh, bless his heart!

He started to whittle a fine wooden chair,
But ended up making a tree's favorite lair.
With no wood for sitting, he let out a sigh,
While birds fluffed their feathers and nearby did fly.

Symphony of the Sylvan Spirits

In the realm of the green, where the sunlight danced,
A fellow with tunes and mischief advanced.
His lute made of bark, with strings made of vine,
Played a tune that made critters not mind the pine.

He'd sing to the trees and they'd sway to his cheer,
With laughter like music that all could hear.
A tumble of logs and a jig in the muck,
He brought joy to the woodland with every pluck.

The Enigma of the Evergreen Clown

In the forest, a joker stands,
With a beard made of leaves so grand.
He tells tales of trees that dance,
And squirrels that love to prance.

With a hat of acorns, tall and wide,
He rides on mushrooms, full of pride.
He tickles the roots and sings to the vine,
While the owls hoot a rhythm divine.

A jolly laugh echoes through the pine,
As critters giggle at his silly line.
He juggles with berries, colors so bright,
Under the moon's shimmering light.

Oh, the chuckles that rise from the trees,
When he performs for the buzzing bees.
In the heart of the woods, he's the star of the show,
Tickling the branches, putting on a glow.

The Whimsical Waltz of Willow and Wind

Among the willows, a dance does take flight,
With breezes that twirl from morning till night.
The branches do sway like they're having a ball,
As laughter and giggles envelop us all.

A rabbit in overalls joins in the fun,
With a tap dance that's second to none.
He hops on the roots with shoes made of dust,
While blossoms all cheer, and we must!

The wind tells a joke that makes the leaves shake,
As the butterflies join in, for goodness' sake.
The flowers all chuckle, their petals aflare,
In a waltz of delight that fills up the air.

When night falls, the glowworms light up the scene,
As the willow's soft whispers blend with the green.
Together they frolic, in shadows and gleam,
In this whimsical waltz, life's a sweet dream.

Echoes of the Enchanted Timber

In the forest, laughter squeals,
A squirrel with shoes, it wheels.
Dancing trees swing like a band,
While mushrooms play in a rock 'n' roll stand.

Breezes hum a silly tune,
With crickets dressed like a cartoon.
Branches sway and giggle along,
Inviting all to join the song.

Secrets of the Sylvan Stroll

A raccoon dons his sun hat bright,
While rabbits hop in pure delight.
The shadows tickle the grass so green,
As whispers float where few have been.

The brook sings tales of mud and clay,
Of funny things that happened today.
Giggling winds carry hoots and cheers,
In a woodland realm where joy adheres.

Whispers from the Woodland Keeper

The keeper winks with a twinkling eye,
As fireflies dance and flicker by.
Acorns giggle, sharing their dreams,
In a world full of funny extremes.

A hedgehog juggles mushrooms round,
While chubby bunnies bounce off the ground.
Squirrels plot their nutty schemes,
As laughter fills the air with beams.

The Jester in the Grove

A jester hops with a cap so bright,
Chasing shadows that dart in flight.
His jests tickle the sleepy trees,
As they're swayed by playful breeze.

With every step, the ground erupts,
In giggles shared, no one is corrupt.
The brook chuckles, the leaves applaud,
For mirth in the grove is the grandest façade.

Beneath the Canopy of Dreams

Silly squirrels play hide and seek,
Chasing shadows, they laugh and squeak.
A rabbit hops in a top hat green,
Juggling acorns with a giggling sheen.

The sun peeks through leaves of jade,
While mushrooms wear cups in a grand parade.
Foxes prance in flamboyant shoes,
Telling tall tales of their crazy blues.

Forest Echoes of Laughter

The raccoon's mask is snug and tight,
He steals the snacks, oh what a sight!
Beneath the boughs, the owl hoots loud,
While crickets chirp, a chirpy crowd.

Bears build castles from logs and twigs,
Bouncing around with wiggly jigs.
A badger juggles shiny stones,
Singing songs in silly tones.

The Dance of the Sylvan Scribe

A mouse in spectacles writes of bliss,
While ladybugs join in the dance's twist.
Each leaf a stage for quirky moves,
In this space where laughter grooves.

The wind whispers secrets full of glee,
As fireflies glow like stars on a spree.
A deer dons a bowtie, all dapper and fine,
He twirls to the rhythm of the forest's rhyme.

Whispers of the Wandering Oak

Tall trees giggle with branches wide,
While critters nuzzle, all filled with pride.
The oak tells tales of paths it's crossed,
In every riddle, there's fun that's tossed.

Rabbits wear glasses made of twine,
Debating the best way to dine.
Bouncing around, they tumble in cheer,
In this woodland, there's nothing to fear.

Portraits of Bark and Bramble

In the forest's cozy nook,
A squirrel wears a fancy crook.
Mice dance round a mushroom's cap,
While badgers take a silly nap.

Trees wear hats of moss and dew,
They giggle as the wind comes through.
With branches stretched like arms so wide,
They tickle each passing woodland bride.

Lanterns of Laughter

Glowworms light the paths we roam,
While frogs sing tunes of happy home.
A rabbit plays a flute made of grass,
While turtles race, but none can pass.

Through foliage laughter echoes clear,
Where critters dance and none show fear.
A party here, no worries near,
Just joy and fun, the atmosphere!

The Secret Life of Stumps

Old stumps whisper tales so grand,
Of secret meetings planned by hand.
With acorns serving as their drink,
They plot and laugh, and who would think?

They argue on the best pizza slice,
While fireflies twinkle, oh so nice!
A fox with glasses takes the lead,
Discussing foliage, that's their creed.

A Guide to Giddy Greenery

If you seek fun among the leaves,
Follow where the sunlight weaves.
You'll find a crowd of giggling trees,
And playful winds that dance with ease.

A guidebook made of bark and cheer,
Awaits you here, so do not fear!
With every step, a chuckle grows,
In the realm where silly nature flows.

The Sway of Spruce Serenades

In a forest where the trees dance,
A lumberjack twirls with his pants askew.
He serenades spruce with a merry glance,
As squirrels laugh and join the hullabaloo.

The branches sway to his quirky tunes,
While the sun peeks through with a cheeky smile.
The critters gather, giving happy croons,
And the woods come alive in silly style.

Chasing Shadows with a Chainsaw

A fella with a chainsaw, quite the sight,
Runs after shadows that twist and shout.
They giggle and dodge with all their might,
Creating mischief as he spins about.

With each rev, the forest holds its breath,
A chorus of giggles fills the air.
He trips on roots, nearly meets his death,
But laughter echoes, banishing despair.

Joyride through the Greenery

On a rickety bike through the leafy maze,
A jovial rider takes awkward turns.
He waves at the critters in a blissful daze,
While a rabbit scampers and brightly burns.

Each bump sends him soaring like a kite,
Over logs and puddles, he takes flight.
Oh, what a sight, with laughter in the air,
As nature joins in this joyful affair.

Finding Glee in the Glades

In the glades where the sunlight breaks,
A gather of friends plays hide and seek.
They tumble and roll with happy aches,
While the trees chuckle, their limbs will creak.

A pie thrown here, a splash over there,
Joyful chaos all around their feet.
They dance like butterflies, without a care,
In the woods, this laughter is oh so sweet.

Giggles in the Grove

In a grove where laughter grew,
Silly squirrels had fun to pursue.
They danced on branches high and low,
And tickled trunks with mischievous woe.

A raccoon wore a hat from straw,
While mockingbirds sang out in awe.
They pranked the trees, they rolled in leaves,
In this grove, no one ever grieves!

With acorns tossed, they played and spun,
Chasing shadows, just for fun.
The sun peeked down to join the cheer,
A giggle echoed, bright and clear!

Amidst the chuckles, the fun would stay,
In the grove where joy led the way.
With every rustle, a joke would rise,
Under the vast, blue, laughing skies.

The Gaudy Gnome's Produce Stand

Underneath a faded tree,
A gnome sells veggies, bright as can be.
His carrots sport polka dots,
While radishes wear silly spots.

With beets in hats and peas that dance,
Each quirky veggie gets a chance.
He juggled cucumbers, lost control,
And let out a big, giggly roll!

The tomatoes winked as he made a deal,
While garlic bulbs shared a cheeky squeal.
"Buy one, get one, just today!"
He shouted in a very odd way.

The gnome's odd stand drew quite a crowd,
And each laugh shared felt a bit loud.
With every sale, he'd wink and grin,
In this market, everyone wins!

Frogs and Folly in the Fern Fronds

Jumping frogs in ferns so green,
Hopping high like a playful dream.
They wore tiny crowns made of leaves,
And practiced their dance with giggly heaves.

With every splash, the pond would cheer,
As frogs leaped high, showing no fear.
A frog in tights twirled around,
While friends made music, a froggy sound!

The dragonflies joined in the glee,
With crazy zips, they flew with spree.
A frog made jokes as if on cue,
"Why did the chicken? Not a clue!"

In the ferns where the laughter flows,
These frogs, they know how fun life goes.
With every croak, a smile ignites,
In their whimsical, carefree nights!

Adventures of the Antlered Artist

A deer with paintbrush in his mouth,
Created art from north to south.
He splashed colors on each tree,
A masterpiece, as wild as can be!

His antlers wore a crown of charms,
While bunnies posed to show their arms.
With every stroke, they struck a pose,
In a gallery where giggles rose.

He painted clouds with buttercream,
A rainbow river, sweet as a dream.
Woodpeckers tapped on every beat,
As critters danced on tiny feet!

"The canvas breathes, come, share a cheer!"
He called to all, "Bring laughter here!"
In the woods, full of whimsy bright,
The artist's joy lit up the night!

Fables from the Forest Floor

In the forest, tales do roam,
Where squirrels share a tiny gnome.
With acorns stacked like tiny hats,
They dance in circles, funny spats.

A rabbit hops while doing the twist,
He's found that carrots are hard to resist.
With a wiggle and a wobble, he takes a bite,
While birds above giggle at the sight.

A bear with honey smeared on his face,
Tries to keep up in a goofy race.
With every step, he slips and slides,
Rolling down hills with arms open wide.

So listen close when the winds do sing,
The forest is full of jests and bling.
Fables bubble up from deep in the floor,
Nature's punchlines, always wanting more.

The Chimney of Cheerful Chopping

There's a lumberjack with a rosy grin,
Who sings to the trees, as he begins.
His axe dances with a jolly clink,
Chopping logs faster than you can blink.

He tells the wood, 'You'd better behave,
Or I'll turn you into a very small grave!'
The pine trees chuckle, they know it's a joke,
For with every swing, they feel not a poke.

A chipmunk threw acorns, what a delight,
While the jack danced under the moonlight.
With a cartwheel of joy, he laughed and spun,
Chopping and cracking, oh what fun!

So if you hike where the green trees sway,
Listen for laughter that lights up the day.
For in the woods with each joyful thump,
You'll find a heart that's forever a jump.

Riddles Among the Roots

Beneath the trees where shadows play,
The roots tell riddles in a silly way.
A wise old toad, with a sly little grin,
Asks the ants "What's the best way to win?"

A squirrel pipes up, "It's simple, you see,
Just gather your nuts, make a grand spree!"
The toad just chuckles, "More than just loot,
It's laughter and fun that roots you to boot."

They argue and giggle, the woods echo jokes,
With mushrooms as seats for the pokey folks.
"I've lost my joke book," the mouse then cries,
"Never fear, just look under the skies!"

So stay a while in their jocular realm,
Where each twist and turn gives laughter the helm.
With riddles and roots that tickle the trees,
The forest whispers secrets with ease.

Joking with the Junipers

Junipers stand with a curious sway,
Throwing out jokes to lighten the day.
"Why did the tree go to school?" they ask,
"To get a little rooted, it's quite the task!"

The bushes giggle, they join in the pun,
"The rabbit who read is always in fun!"
As leaves shake silently, efforts unite,
In the shade where all things feel light.

An owl hoots loud, "I'm wise, oh so wise,
But I can't tell jokes without a disguise!"
A cap and a tie, he looks real swell,
"It's the hoot of the hour, you can't tell!"

So in this wild place where laughter does bloom,
With junipers chuckling, chaos does loom.
If you wander here, with laughter explore,
You'll never feel lonely, the jokes will soar.

Tales from the Timbered Realm

Once a tree wore a silly hat,
The squirrels giggled and said, "What's that?"
With leaves as ribbons, it danced around,
The laughter echoed, a joyous sound.

A rabbit decided to join the fun,
His ears flopped up, like a morning sun.
He twirled and hopped with great delight,
While birds chirped songs of pure delight.

A fox in boots pranced near the brook,
With a can-do charm that no one mistook.
He juggled acorns, dropped them with flair,
As all the critters stopped to stare.

In such a place where all could play,
They'd dawdle and loiter, all night and day.
A merry menagerie in the glen,
Where laughter sparkled like dew once again.

A Robin's Riddle in the Glade

A robin sang, perched high on a limb,
With tales of nuts and acorn whim.
"What comes at dusk but flies all day?"
"Just listen close to what I say!"

The critters gathered, both big and small,
They leaned in close, they wanted it all.
A hedgehog guessed, then fell fast asleep,
While the wise old owl began to peep.

"Is it a breeze or the stars' bright eyes?"
The chatter grew, with puzzled sighs.
"What tricks reside in the woods so dear?"
The robin just chuckled, "You've got it near!"

At last, came the answer, bright as the sun,
"It's laughter, my friends! Now wasn't that fun?"
With a wink and a hop, she started to fly,
Leaving behind echoes of questions awry.

The Jester among the Trees

A jester arrived with a laugh and a jig,
Wearing bright colors, just one little fig.
He cartwheeled past, making all the leaves sway,
As laughter bubbled like fresh morning spray.

With tricks and pranks, he tugged at some tails,
The owls rolled their eyes, sharing their tales.
He wore a grin that was quite out of place,
Upon the face of a woodland's embrace.

A dance-off ensued on a log by the way,
Where beetles competed with flair for the day.
With bells that jingled, the pranks took their turn,
To frolic and tease—oh, how their hearts burned!

As dusk fell gently and shadows grew long,
The jester bowed low, singing his song.
In every corner echoed the glee,
As moonlight twinkled on this wild spree.

Mirth by the Mossy Boughs

Beneath the boughs, where shadows play,
A gathering formed at the end of the day.
The frogs croaked jokes in a giggling spree,
While mushrooms giggled in silent glee.

A turtle told tales of speedy delight,
While a butterfly swooped, dancing in light.
The bobbling brook chimed with every guffaw,
The woodland erupted in laughter's sweet draw.

With moss for seats and bark for a stage,
The critters enacted their own frolic page.
The oddest of friends, all gathered around,
In a symphony of joy, no frowns to be found.

As night wrapped the woods in a silvery veil,
The laughter still hummed, a whimsical trail.
By the mossy boughs where the magic was spun,
Their hearts were forever in mirth undone.

A Cradle of Curious Creatures

In a nook of the glade, they chuckle and play,
Furry faces peeking, brightening day.
A rabbit with glasses reads tales from a tome,
While squirrels on stilts parade through the loam.

A hedgehog in socks twirls under the sun,
Reciting wild rhymes, they giggle and run.
With each rustle and roar, mirth fills the air,
A circus of woodland friends beyond compare.

The owls share gossip in whispers, not loud,
While a porcupine juggles, drawing a crowd.
The giggling fawns dance in circles quite neat,
While raccoons play drums with an upbeat beat.

In this cradle of laughter, all worries are few,
For here in the woods, joy blossoms anew.
So join in their frolic, don't miss the fun,
In this enchanted forest, there's laughter for everyone.

Barking Up the Right Tree

Under the branches, a ruckus unfolds,
As a parrot's backstory hilariously told.
A bear in a cap tries to dance with a hare,
While the raccoon's sly eyes plot tricks in the air.

A woodpecker drums with a rhythm so fine,
While a squirrel seeks acorns, claiming them mine.
All creatures gather, their spirits so high,
Cackles and howls fill the underwood sky.

The lizard does flips on a sun-warmed log,
And a badger performs with a fine froggy fog.
Join in the chorus, let laughter take flight,
For a tale of the woods is a joyful delight!

So if you're feeling low, take a stroll through the trees,
Barking up laughter brings hearts to their knees.
In this merry old thicket, they teach us to play,
And life is much brighter when we laugh every day.

Spinning Tales in Twisted Limbs

In the twisting branches where shadows reside,
A fox shares wild stories, half-mischief, and pride.
He spins them like webs; his eyes glimmer bright,
As the crowd of odd creatures leans in with delight.

A turtle in boots plays the part of a king,
While a wily old raccoon pulls pranks on a string.
From tales of adventures to legends of old,
Each tale gets more fanciful, funny, and bold.

With owls all a-hoot and toads croaking cheers,
The air crackles with joy and a sprinkle of jeers.
A badger narrates with dramatic flair,
The antics of critters who frolic with care.

So gather around where the stories unfold,
With magic and laughter, it's pure joy to behold.
In the grove where the shadows and giggles align,
Every whimsical story adds sparkle and shine.

The Joyful Journey of Timber

Off on an adventure, our brave logs all cheer,
With twigs armed with laughter, there's nothing to fear.
From puddles to boulders, they bounce and they sway,
In a fanciful parade, they dance every day.

With barked-out laughter, they roll down the slope,
Creating wild shadows and givers of hope.
The pinecones act silly, the acorns declare,
That laughter is better when shared, in the air.

Split wood makes a jest, "Let's tell a tall tale!"
And fashion a party right under the gale.
Moss joins the beat with a jitterbug twist,
While sunbeams join in and couldn't resist.

From sapling to elder, they share every grin,
In the joyful journey, it's fun to join in.
Through gnarled and green timber, so merry and bright,
With each playful moment, they glow in delight.

Tap Dance on the Trunk

In the woods where the trees sway,
A fellow prances night and day.
With tap shoes made of acorn hats,
He dances here, he dances that!

The squirrels stop to see his show,
They chuckle loud, they holler 'Whooa!'
With every step the ground does thump,
His rhythm makes the forest jump!

The owls hoot with delight so bright,
As shadows twirl in the moonlight.
With every clap, the leaves all cheer,
A merry tune for all to hear!

So if you stroll past the old oak,
Look closer, friend, it's not a joke!
A tap-dancing bard, with friends in tow,
In the woods where giggles grow!

Whimsical Whittlings

With a tiny knife and a playful grin,
A fellow sits where the tales begin.
He carves up creatures, oh what a scene,
From chubby frogs to a playful queen!

Each chip of wood flies with glee,
Little critters come to see.
A whittled fish goes flop and flop,
While daisies giggle, 'Please don't stop!'

The rabbits clap in their fluffy coats,
As the whimsical woodman clearly floats.
With every whittle, magic's found,
A treasure trove on the forest ground!

So if you see a twinkle bright,
Just know it's wood chips taking flight.
And in the air, the laughter sings,
Of whimsical men and their funny things!

The Frolicking Fir

In a forest full of play and cheer,
A fir tree sways with a funny leer.
He shakes his branches, what a sight!
Dancing with glee under the moonlight!

With pinecone hats and acorn shoes,
The fir tree jives without a bruise.
He twirls with bunnies, skips with deer,
Making merry, spreading cheer!

A playful breeze joins in the fun,
As shadows dance, oh what a run!
The critters gather, laughter abounds,
In the funky rhythm of nature's sounds!

When night falls soft and stars do gleam,
The frolicking fir begins to dream.
Of silly dances and woodland tunes,
Under the gaze of smiling moons!

Skits in the Sylvan Scene

Amidst the trees, the antics fly,
A band of creatures, oh me, oh my!
The rabbit tricks and the fox's dance,
In the sylvan scene, they take a chance!

The raccoons juggle with pinecone balls,
While the deer laugh hard at their silly falls.
A chorus of hoots, a tittering sound,
Nature's comedy knows no bound!

The owls serve popcorn, flicking with glee,
As the forest stage blooms, a sight to see.
The show goes on 'til the stars take stage,
Each act unravels with fun and rage!

So stroll on by, don't pass it up,
Join in the laughter, grab a cup!
For in this wood, the silliness reigns,
With skits and giggles in joyful chains.

The Enigma of Evergreen

In the forest where oddities grow,
Trees wear hats, don't you know?
Squirrels dance in silly tights,
While mushrooms host tea parties at night.

The owls play chess with the moon,
Their laughter echoes a playful tune.
Breezes tickle the branches high,
As acorns drop from a giggling sky.

A fox wearing glasses reads a book,
Underneath a bright, shiny nook.
With every turn of the page he grins,
While raccoons join in for some spins.

So wander here where laughter flows,
In this place where laughter grows.
For in the woods of curious cheer,
Every nook has a charm so dear.

A Whirlwind among the Willows

A dance begins in soft embrace,
With branches swaying in folly's grace.
Willows whisper their secrets low,
While ladybugs drum on to and fro.

A dandy deer dons a silly hat,
"Come one, come all!" he says with a spat.
The creek joins in with a gurgling laugh,
As crickets invite with notes on their staff.

Frogs try on shoes that spark and gleam,
While snails form a line in a race-like dream.
Nature giggles, a jester's delight,
As lightning bugs dance in flickering light.

Here in the whirlwind, fun never ends,
With willow whispers and joyful bends.
So venture near, don't take a pass,
For laughter sparkles like dew on grass.

Play in the Pinecone Paradise

In a realm where pinecones have their say,
They roll and tumble, come out to play.
Bouncing gently off mossy beds,
Where giggling whispers fill little heads.

Chipmunks juggle with berries round,
As pine needles dance on the ground.
Sunbeams shimmer through branches wide,
As laughter echoes along with the tide.

A party of creatures in a grand parade,
With squirrels, and rabbits, and songs that are laid.
Each tree a stage in this comedy show,
With giggles and wiggles as soft breezes blow.

So come to the pines, bring your glee,
Join the frolic, be wild, be free.
For every day here is a bright surprise,
In the playtime haven, beneath sunny skies.

The Twilight Troupe of Trees

As dusk paints the sky in twinkling threads,
The trees gather round, in their wooden beds.
An owl in a bowtie takes the lead,
While whispers of laughter mingle with speed.

The firs tap dance on their sturdy roots,
While the maples sway in their vibrant suits.
With fireflies lighting the stage away,
It's a riot of fun in the fading day.

A troupe of shadows, with giggles that rise,
Sprinkle fairy dust from bright, starry skies.
The wind plays a tune with a chuckling breeze,
As stars drop down, full of playful tease.

So join the performance, join in the fun,
When twilight wraps all in a hug and a pun.
For in this grove, where the shadows convene,
Magic lives and mischief is seen.

Medley of Merrymaking in the Mesquite

In the mesquite there's a dance,
A lass with shoes of wildest chance.
Her hat is tipped, her smile so wide,
While critters chuckle, oh, so spry.

With squirrels prancing, acorns fly,
As jigs and jests sweep through the sky.
A toucan sings its silly tune,
Underneath the grinning moon.

The cactus nods with cactus flair,
While lizards leap without a care.
All twirl and spin, what a delight,
In this grove of sheer respite.

When the sun dips low, the laughter swells,
Echoing through the woodland spells.
In playful chaos, they'll remain,
The mesquite's heart is full of gain.

The Trickster's Tapestry in the Trees

In the trees, a jester's show,
With tricks and pranks that steal the glow.
A beaver wears a bright red tie,
As owls hoot softly from way up high.

A raccoon dons a mask so sly,
While he plots another pie in the sky.
The branches shake with giggles light,
As shadows dance, an amusing sight.

Fibers of laughter woven tight,
A tapestry of pure delight.
Squirrels swing on a rope so grand,
Pulling pranks on all the land.

Under the canopy's playful grasp,
The forest holds each laugh like a clasp.
For here, the mischief knows no bounds,
In nature's theater, joy resounds.

Portrait of a Playful Sapling

In a clearing, a sapling stands,
With wavy branches, flappy hands.
It sways and giggles in the sun,
A little tree that knows how to run.

Crickets chirp a merry tune,
As butterflies play hopscotch at noon.
The sapling twirls in the gentle breeze,
What a sight, to laugh with ease.

Worms parade in festive lines,
While beetles boast of silly times.
The sapling tries a funny pose,
As sunlight dances on its nose.

And when the storm clouds start to form,
It spreads its leaves, determined, warm.
With a wink, it shakes off the gloom,
This sprightly sprout will always bloom.

Fables of Frost and Frivolity

In the frosty woods where giggles spread,
The snowflakes dance on a jester's bed.
A rabbit sports a coat of white,
Holding court in the chilly night.

With icicles hanging like little swords,
The woodland critters hatch new chords.
A frosty fox, so slick and sly,
Chasing dreams that float on by.

The tales are spun with snowy grace,
Where every flake finds its own place.
Together they giggle, jump, and play,
In their capricious, winter ballet.

As dawn breaks with a frosty grin,
The woods awake, new fun begins.
Each fable shared amidst the frost,
Brings joy multiplied, never lost.

Laughter Beneath the Canopy

In the woods where giggles play,
A squirrel juggles nuts all day.
He slips and trips, a clumsy feat,
With acorns landing at my feet.

The owls wear glasses, wise but funny,
Debating over which fruit is honey.
They hoot and laugh, a comic script,
While little bunnies dance and skipped.

A bear who thinks he can ballet,
Twirls and tumbles in a silly way.
The forest echoes with a roar,
As trees shake hands and spirits soar.

The sun peeks through, a playful tease,
Lighting up the dancing leaves.
Each shadow winks, each twig does grin,
In the meadow's laughter, we all spin.

Frolics with the Forest Phantom

A ghost with a grin, so full of cheer,
Pops out from behind a tree so near.
His jokes are old, but they're quite spry,
He tickles my ribs and makes me cry.

We chase fireflies racing through the glade,
His silly antics never do fade.
He slips on leaves with a comic squeal,
And spins for fun, it's quite a deal.

With dandelions, we blow puffy seeds,
Turning whispers into playful deeds.
The forest hums a jolly tune,
As we frolic beneath the laughing moon.

In every crook, a story glows,
The phantom shows what nobody knows.
With a wink and a cheer, he bids adieu,
Leaving behind laughter anew.

Starlit Tales of the Tree Tamer

Under the stars, a tall tale spins,
Of a man who dances with furry twins.
He teaches foxes how to juggle,
While raccoons laugh and start to snuggle.

The moonlight sparkles on his cap,
A mix of colors, quite a flap!
With whispered tales, the owls gather 'round,
Amid the chuckles, magic's found.

The napping pines hold secrets tight,
But with his charm, they burst with delight.
He tickles the branches, making them sway,
Turning the night into a playful ballet.

With twinkling dreams, the creatures cheer,
While laughter echoes, drawing near.
In starlit magic, joy takes flight,
In the woods, we dance with pure delight.

Bark and Blossom: A Phantasm

In a glen where giggles bloom,
A tree with bark spreads laughs, not gloom.
His branches sway to a funny rhyme,
As blossoms giggle in perfect time.

A hedgehog rolls in a polka-dot coat,
While bumblebees hum, their sweet little note.
The mushrooms join in a wobbly dance,
It's a raucous party, not left to chance.

The daisies chime like cheerful bells,
While woodland critters cast funny spells.
Each rustling leaf is a whispered joke,
A jubilant sigh beneath the oak.

As dusk draws near, the fun won't cease,
The woods embrace us, wrapping in peace.
With a wink from the night, the laughter streams,
In this enchanted space, we chase our dreams.

Folklore of the Fertile Glade

In a glade where laughter plays,
Trees wear hats made of sunbeams.
Squirrels dance in a silly craze,
Whispering all their wild dreams.

Mushrooms chat with the passing breeze,
Winking secrets all around.
A raccoon, with mischief, aims to tease,
As his antics abound and abound.

Bees in bow ties buzz with cheer,
Playing tag with the filtering light.
A frog croaks jokes to all who hear,
As shadows twist into the night.

In this land of chortles and chases,
Where old trees tell tales with glee.
Nature wears hilarious faces,
In the heart of the jolly spree.

The Parable of Prancing Pines

Tall pines in a grand ballet,
Twist and twirl with flouncy flair.
They sway and bow, come what may,
Dancing gracefully in the air.

A woodpecker beats a funky tune,
Inviting all to join the fun.
Rabbits hop under the moon,
While everyone's laughing on the run.

With every twist, a giggle grows,
As branches tickle the fluffy clouds.
In this forest, joy simply flows,
Tickling grumps from their proud shrouds.

In this parable, smiles always shine,
As nature's rhythm plays its part.
So let the pines teach your heart,
That joy and laughter intertwine.

Mysteries of the Marbled Maples

In a land where colors collide,
Maples wear coats of striped delight.
They giggle as they try to hide,
From squirrels who play games at night.

Every leaf a vivid mystery,
With whispers soft like summer's breath.
They share jokes, and history,
'Till the dawn comes to steal their depth.

A chipmunk juggles acorns up high,
While owls hoot their curious plight.
The maples spin tales as they sigh,
In the soft glow of moonlit night.

Together they spin their lore,
Making mischief with each turn.
From roots to branches, tales galore,
In the woods, there's much to learn.

The Colorful Capers of Citrus Cedars

Cedars dressed in citrus hues,
Laugh aloud with zesty charm.
Lemons giggle, as if on cue,
"Don't let life lose its sweet alarm!"

They swagger with a playful flair,
While limes roll in jesting rounds.
Chasing shadows without a care,
As laughter in the air abounds.

Every branch exudes a tease,
Each tree's a jester in the grove.
Ripe fruits sway with breezes that please,
In this place where all weird paths rove.

Together in this playful space,
Cedars and citrus blend with ease.
In the heart of their vibrant grace,
Joy erupts like colorful pleas.

The Unruly Man of the Thicket

In a thicket so dense, he roams with a grin,
Chasing shadows and squirrels, where mischief begins.
He fumbles with branches, ties knots in his shoelaces,
And wears mismatched socks that are true to their places.

With a hat made of leaves and a coat full of mud,
He dances with rabbits, twirls logs in the flood.
He tries to catch fireflies with a wildly thrown net,
But somehow trips over the very same pet.

His laughter rings loud through the chirps of the night,
Convincing the owls to join in the fright.
With a wiggle and jiggle, he invites them to play,
But they hoot and then vanish, just fading away.

For he's quite the oddball, a sight to behold,
A ruckus in nature, with stories retold.
And each time he stumbles, the woods come alive,
With giggles and whispers, they dance and they thrive.

A Dance with the Sylph of Saplings

In glimmer and glamour, she twirls 'neath the trees,
A dance with the shadows, a jig in the breeze.
He joins in the frolic, all spry and unplanned,
But steps on a twig that he never had spanned.

The saplings are laughing, they bow and they sway,
Encouraging him for a quirky ballet.
But tangled in roots, he spins round and round,
While the sylph in her splendor giggles, spellbound.

He pirouettes past, with a bark and a thud,
And lands in a patch where the soft moss is bud.
With a wink and a whistle, he finds his next chance,
To show the whole forest his wild, wobbly dance.

In the moonlight so bright, the stars start to hum,
As he trips and he tops, and he bangs like a drum.
The sylph shakes her head, yet can't help but smile,
As he stumbles and giggles, his foolishly style.

Riddles Among the Rustic Roots

Beneath tangled branches, he grins with delight,
Crafting riddles for critters that dart through the night.
"What has keys but can't open the door?" he will jest,
The squirrels pause their scurrying, pondering the quest.

"Why do trees ask for a little more wood?"
They chuckle, they cheer, as he answers for good.
With giggles erupting, they share in the fun,
Chasing after their thoughts 'til the riddle is done.

"Why did the mushroom go party alone?"
He quips with a chuckle, then starts to enthrone.
The jesters and jays gather 'round for a laugh,
Combining their wits for a whimsical craft.

Through rustling leaves, he sparkles with glee,
Creating wild stories near tall, wavy trees.
As dawn starts to break, they all bid adieu,
Till next time he gathers with riddles anew.

The Mischief Maker of Mossy Caverns

In a cavern of moss, where the shadows all play,
A fellow with mischief stirs up the day.
He tickles the stalactites, they giggle and shake,
And the echoes join in, for goodness' sweet sake.

With bubbles of laughter, he leaps with a bound,
Flings pebbles at toads, who hop wildly around.
Chasing flashes of light that flit to and fro,
Finding joy in the chaos, with nowhere to go.

The rocks roll and tumble, they join in the spree,
As bright-eyed creatures peek out, curious to see.
He crafts little traps made of twigs and bright leaves,
To catch all the chuckles that float 'neath the eaves.

When twilight arrives, and the fun starts to fade,
He whispers his secrets whilst laughter parades.
For in caverns of moss, where mischief runs free,
He's the chortling spirit of light-hearted glee.

Mischief in the Maple Grove

In a grove where trees wear crowns so green,
A fellow pranks with glee, seldom seen.
He ties some branches in a dance so wild,
Leaves laughing, nature's mischievous child.

Squirrels giggle as they leap and play,
His tricks unfold in a most curious way.
With acorns flying through the sunlit air,
Our jester hides behind a leafy lair.

The birds chirp tunes, playful and spry,
While shadows twist as they flit and fly.
Each step he takes, a silly little skip,
In this funny wood, he won't lose his grip.

As twilight falls and stars start to peek,
All cheer for the fun, for the laughter's unique.
In the maple grove, where giggles reside,
A merry heart dances, there's joy far and wide.

The Journey of a Joyful Timber

Once a log with a smile so bright,
Rolls down a hill, oh what a sight!
Bouncing and tumbling—a wobbly spree,
Shouting to friends, 'Come roll with me!'

Through the forest, he bounces, no fear,
With chipmunks cheering, oh what a cheer!
Past mushrooms that giggle and flowers that grin,
Each hop an adventure, let the fun begin!

He meets a wise owl, perched sky high,
Who joins in the fun with a twinkling eye.
'Let's all be merry, and dance in the breeze!'
The log rolls on with laughter and ease.

At the creek, he splashes, oh what a mess,
But joy in the woods is what he loves best.
With friends all around, laughter fills the air,
Our joyful timber spreads cheer everywhere!

Dance of the Daring Druid

In the heart of the woods under moon's soft glow,
A daring druid dances, putting on a show.
With leaves as his partners and stars in his eyes,
He twirls through the night, beneath starlit skies.

He hops over roots and he zigs 'n' zags,
Each step is a giggle, each turn a brag.
Frogs join the rhythm, their croaks a delight,
In a merry celebration that lasts through the night.

The night critters laugh and tap their tiny toes,
As the druid spins more with each graceful pose.
Mushrooms start swaying, caught up in the cheer,
While fireflies blink in appreciation here.

With a final flourish, he bows to the crowd,
An uproar of smiles, so joyful and loud.
In the dance of the druid, the woods come alive,
With laughter and light, oh how they thrive!

A Nutty Adventure in the Underbrush

In the underbrush where pesky squirrels play,
A nutty adventure unfolds every day.
With acorns a-flying, they giggle and cheer,
As they race through the grass with nothing to fear.

Two buddies decide to make the best stash,
They gather up nuts in an enthusiastic dash.
But oops! They trip over a log on the way,
It's a bonkers tumble—oh, what a display!

They shake off the leaves and start once again,
Plotting their course like heroes, with zen.
A treasure hunt sounds like such an affair,
With friends by their side and adventures to share!

Among thorns and vines, their giggles grow loud,
Chasing bright butterflies, feeling so proud.
Every nook in the brush is filled with delight,
In this nutty escapade, joy takes flight!

The Unexpected Adventures in Green Shadows

In shadows deep where giggles grow,
A hat's askew, a squirrel's in tow.
They dance and twirl, a comical sight,
Beneath the moon's soft, silver light.

A jumping jack with trunk so wide,
Tripped on a log, fell with pride.
The birds all cackled, what a scene!
In the forest, joy is evergreen.

With each new step, a laugh erupts,
Even the trees join in the hiccups.
A rhyming brook sings songs of cheer,
While mischievous shadows lurk near.

So skip along, let worries fade,
In this lush land of jests well-made.
Embrace the strange, the silly, the fun,
For every adventure has just begun.

A Song of Twigs and Tinkling Laughter

Twigs are playing in a merry band,
With tiny drums and a tickling hand.
A chorus of chuckles fills the air,
As branches sway without a care.

Laughter bubbles from the bubbling brook,
While Ladybugs dance and tiny worms look.
The sunbeams peek through leaves up high,
Making the heart soar and sigh.

Whispers of joy beneath the ferns,
And every nook and cranny churns.
A celebration of life, wild and free,
In a symphony of jests, just you and me.

So join the mayhem, be a part,
With every chuckle, we steal a heart.
From morning's light to evening's glow,
This woodland's laughter will ever flow.

Echoes of Dreaming Pines

In pines that sway with tales untold,
A whisper floats, both warm and bold.
Echoes giggle like a child's sweet dream,
As cackling critters plot a scheme.

A rogue raccoon with mischief planned,
Juggles acorns with a steady hand.
While fireflies blink in a silly dance,
The pines sway gently, in a trance.

Mushrooms sprout with colorful glee,
Throwing a party for the great oak tree.
Each furred and feathered friend takes part,
In this woodland circus, bursting with heart.

As shadows stretch and night unfolds,
The laughter lingers, a treasure of gold.
With every step, a new giggle finds,
The secrets kept by dreaming pines.

The Unseen Friend in the Ferns

Amongst the ferns, a giggle hides,
An unseen friend, where mischief bides.
With every rustle, a secret's spilled,
As nature's wonders are gently thrilled.

A crabby caterpillar throws a fit,
About a twig that wouldn't fit.
While butterflies flutter, spreading cheer,
The unseen friend is always near.

Jolly toads play games of peek,
With shadows soft as they softly speak.
A riddle here, a puzzle there,
In ferns and fronds, there's magic to share.

So embrace the mirth, let laughter unfold,
In the whispers of ferns, stories are told.
With every chuckle that dances around,
The unseen friend is joyfully found.

Playful Patterns in the Pines

In the pines where shadows dance,
Squirrels prance in a wild trance.
Raccoons wear hats made of leaves,
While the owl giggles, never grieves.

Twirling trees with burly branches,
Catch the wind in silly stances.
Bunnies hop in polka dots,
Chasing dreams in jolly spots.

Gnarled roots play peek-a-boo,
Tickling toes of the passing crew.
A brook sings tunes of playful glee,
As frogs in ties sip herbal tea.

So if you wander through this place,
Expect a smile on every face.
Nature laughs, you can't ignore,
Adventure waits behind each door.

Mischief Beneath the Ferns

Under ferns where giggles hide,
Mice in capes take a joyride.
A fox juggles acorns with flair,
While an ant wears a tiny chair.

Beneath the leaves, the mischief grows,
Bunnies dance in polka clothes.
Lizards buzzing like tiny cars,
Running races with light-up stars.

Toads hold court in a grassy glen,
Singing songs with a raucous zen.
Bumblebees in tutus spin,
Creating chaos — let the fun begin!

In this patch of leafy cheer,
Laughter rings from ear to ear.
Join the fun, don't be late,
Mischief awaits — it's just our fate.

Songs of Sap and Smiles

Saplings sing in sweet delight,
As the sun sets, painting the night.
Woodpeckers tap a cheerful beat,
While chipmunks dance on little feet.

A squirrel tells a joke that's grand,
"Why did the acorn take a stand?"
The answer floats on the evening breeze,
As laughter bubbles through the trees.

It's a carnival of chirps and whirs,
Where every critter happily stirs.
With pinecone hats and twigs for wands,
They conjure spells of giggles and gronds.

So in the woods where the bubble streams flow,
Songs intertwine with smiles aglow.
Join the choir, let joy be your guide,
In this melody of nature, abide.

Whimsy in the Wildwood

In the wildwood where dreams abound,
Whimsical wonders can be found.
A starlit path of twirling light,
Guides the way through the magical night.

Fluffy clouds sport silly grins,
Butterflies spin in bright, zany spins.
The grass tickles feet as you run,
While daisies chuckle, just having fun.

A tiny troll brews leafy stew,
For fairies dancing in skies so blue.
The punchline's hidden in every twist,
Join the laughter — you won't want to miss!

So skip along and take a chance,
In this place of whimsical dance.
With every step, let joy ignite,
In the wildwood, hearts take flight.

A Dance with the Dappled Sun

Beneath the trees, he twirls with glee,
Frolicking freely, like a bumblebee.
Sunbeams flicker, a golden show,
He trips on roots, and down he goes!

Squirrels giggle from high above,
As he stumbles, they shout with love.
He dusts off leaves, gives a playful pout,
Then swings his arms and shouts, "Look out!"

Laughter echoes through the boughs,
A clumsy prince, he takes his bows.
Butterflies flutter, wide-eyed and bold,
At this jester in the woods, oh so gold!

The sunlight dances, shadows play,
A merry romp in the woods each day.
To chase the beams and sing with cheer,
He brings the forest joy, oh dear!

Dreams Among the Dandelions

In a field of fluff, he takes a seat,
With dandelions blooming at his feet.
He plucks a stem, gives it a blow,
Sending wishes where the soft winds blow.

Dancing spores, like tiny stars,
He strikes a pose, mimicking cars.
"Vroom! Vroom!" he shouts, with a grand old grin,
Cacti and daisies cheer him as he spins.

Ladybugs laugh, his companions in fun,
As he rides on grass blades, under the sun.
A tumble and roll turn into a race,
Chasing the fluff, oh, what a chase!

With soil-stained hands, he crafts a crown,
Dandelions bright in his floral gown.
He bows to the daisies, takes a prance,
And twirls with joy in his whimsical dance!

Whimsy and Wonder in the Wilderness

In the heart of the woods, where the wild things play,
A jester springs forth, both goofy and sway.
He wears a hat, with acorns adorned,
A silly sight, that leaves laughter spawned.

With a leap and a skip, he charms the creek,
Making fish giggle and turtles squeak.
"Why so serious?" he beams with delight,
As he juggles pebbles in broad daylight!

A riddle for snails, a dance for the ants,
He hosts wild parties, and all creatures prance.
Mushrooms shake hands, in a fanciful way,
While the breeze whispers secrets of the day.

Chasing his shadow, a whimsical race,
He tumbles and rolls, leaves a funny trace.
In this treasure of nature, full of cheer,
He finds the magic that lives far and near!

The Puns of Ponderosa

A tall tree named Pine, found humor so fine,
With jokes about bark, and sap that can shine.
Amongst the Ponderosa, he threw out a pun,
From sunrise's giggles to the set of the sun.

"I'm kind of sappy," he chuckled with flair,
As the chipmunks snickered and joined in the air.
"Tree-mendously funny," they shouted with glee,
While the owls hooted from their perch on a spree.

When lightning struck, he shouted, "That's shocking!"
The forest erupted, with laughter unlocking.
With each witty jest, the trees swayed in tune,
While the squirrels danced under the light of the moon.

As dusk settled in, the laughter still soared,
Pine winked at the stars, with puns well explored.
In the heart of the woods, laughter was spry,
With humor to share, from the earth to the sky!

Songs of the Singing Sapling

In the grove where shadows dance,
Saplings sing their silly prance,
Raccoons in top hats tap their feet,
As squirrels spin tales, oh what a feat!

Frogs croak sweetly, leader of the band,
With a lollipop mic in a webbed hand,
Beetles glide with a zany twist,
While everyone giggles, oh, who could resist?

A wobbly owl joins the choir,
In a frock coat of feathers inspired,
Branches sway to the merry beat,
While laughter blooms, oh what a treat!

So come, take a walk where the sillies play,
Where every leaf has its own cabaret,
Among laughing trees, let your worries go,
In the jolly woods where the weirdos glow!

Characters in the Canopy

In the thick of green, a nutty crowd,
Parrots squawk, and laughter's loud,
A dapper skunk with a scented flair,
Offers acorns, with a wink and a stare.

Giggling fawns in polka dot dresses,
Prance around without any stresses,
A hedgehog juggles berries with grace,
While porcupines dance in a prickly race.

A wise old turtle, slow and wise,
Sells lemonade with a twinkle in his eyes,
His secret recipe from days of yore,
Is the talk of the woods, who could ask for more?

From the tallest branch to the smallest root,
Each character knows how to cut a hoot,
In the fun-filled zone of leafy surprise,
Where every day brings a brand-new guise!

The Joy and Jest of Jinglewood

In Jinglewood, where laughter rings,
The trees wear hats and the brook sings,
A jolly deer prances on the trail,
With ribbons tied on his vibrant tail.

Bunnies bake in a cozy nook,
Whipping up treats from their favorite book,
A pie contest held beneath moonlight,
With judges of owls that can't quite take flight.

Frolicsome foxes tell tales so tall,
Of adventures that baffle and enthrall,
Each word a giggle, each laugh a cheer,
As they sip "grass smoothies" and share their beer!

So come join the fun in this merry space,
Where every glance brings a smiling face,
In the joyful woods where no one feels blue,
Jinglewood's antics are waiting for you!

Rhapsody of the Rambling Ranger

A ranger roams with a feathered hat,
Who trades sharp axes for a petting cat,
His compass spins, for it loves a jest,
Leading him to places of laughter's nest.

With a grin that rivals the moonlit sky,
He prances past trees, oh so spry,
Each path he takes is a giggle parade,
With beavers who build a water slide cascade!

Banging on drums made of hollow logs,
Jamborees bring all the wiggle-wogs,
A panda in boots plays a banjo loud,
Creating a ruckus to draw in the crowd.

In this woodland realm, joy knows no bounds,
Where laughter and songs can always be found,
So follow the ranger with joyful cheer,
For whimsy awaits whenever he's near!

A Willow's Witty Refrain

In the shade of leafy dreams,
A joke slips through sunbeams.
Willow whispers with a grin,
"Why do tree stumps never win?"

Squirrels chuckle, branches sway,
As the old trunk starts to play.
Each leaf dances, light and free,
Sharing laughs with bumblebees.

Rabbits hop, their ears a-twitch,
"What did the acorn say? A glitch!"
Beneath the sky, so bright and blue,
Nature laughs, and so should you!

So gather round, friends from afar,
Listen close to the loony spar.
In this grove, where giggles grow,
Joyful tales continue to flow.

Secrets of the Secluded Glen

In a glen where giggles bloom,
Secrets hide amidst the gloom.
What did the flower sing today?
"I'm not a weed, I'm on display!"

The mushrooms dance in polka dots,
Telling tales of silly thoughts.
"Why did the twig cross the stream?"
"To show off in a woodland dream!"

A raccoon juggles forest fruits,
While owls wear the silliest boots.
Laughter fills the air so sweet,
As critters gather for a treat.

Secrets shared and jokes exchanged,
In this place where fun is ranged.
Nature's laughter, wild and free,
Its bountiful joy, a jubilee!

Frolics in Forest's Embrace

Underneath the leafy dome,
Creatures frolic, far from home.
"How do trees keep their hair bright?"
"With a shampoo for pine, just right!"

Sassy squirrels leap and twirl,
While dancing leaves give a whirl.
A bear joins in with a silly jig,
Prompting laughs, both loud and big.

Frogs croak out their latest tune,
In the light of the playful moon.
"What's a tree's favorite number?"
"Root ten, now that's a cucumber!"

Joy and jokes in the sun's warm glow,
Nature's comedy has its flow.
So come and join this lively race,
In the forest's carefree space!

The Enchanted Ax

In a clearing, bright and spry,
An ax swings with a winked eye.
"Why did the wood say, 'Take my weight'?"
"Because I'm too log to contemplate!"

The ax chuckles, bright with glee,
Chopping jokes for all to see.
"What did one log say to the other?"
"Let's roll along, you lumber brother!"

Woodpeckers join the quirky fun,
Pecking out beats, one by one.
"Why don't trees ever get lost?"
"Because they know the path at all cost!"

So swing with laughter, join the show,
In the woods where witticisms flow.
Nature's charm and humor blend,
Crafting joy without end!

A Puppet Show of Petal and Pine

In the glade where shadows dance,
A puppeteer gives laughter a chance.
With flowers and twigs, he strings them high,
As squirrels clap paws; oh my, oh my!

A leaf tumbles down with a giggling cheer,
While butterflies whisper, 'Come look over here!'
The moss beneath wiggles, tickled by glee,
As a show of whimsy bursts forth from the tree.

Secrets Hidden in the Thicket

Behind the brambles, a secret was found,
A raccoon in costume, spinning around.
He juggles acorns while the owl hoots,
In this leafy circus of furry recruits.

The hedgehogs chuckle, in prickly delight,
At the jester who twirls in the soft moonlight.
But with a loud FOOF, he trips on a root,
Sending the audience into a hoot!

Revelry of the Rustling Leaves

The leaves decided to throw a grand ball,
With wind as the DJ to beckon them all.
In twirls and flips, they danced with such flair,
Creating a whirl that tickled the air.

A fox snuck in wearing a grand old hat,
Adding to the laughter with a dance and a cat.
They spun and they laughed until morning light,
A revelry born from the whispering night.

Tapestry of Twisted Boughs

Upon the boughs, a tale is spun,
Of twigs and branches, all having fun.
A spider plays tricks with a web like a joke,
While the raccoon giggles, it's all just smoke.

An owl nearby rolls its big wide eyes,
At the antics of friends where absurdity lies.
From knot to knot, they swing and they sway,
In this tapestry bright, where silliness plays.

www.ingramcontent.com/pod-product-compliance
Lightning Source LLC
Chambersburg PA
CBHW071853160426
43209CB00003B/530